THE FIRST
AMERICAN NOVELIST?

Courtesy of Barton Collection, Boston Public Library

CHARLOTTE LENNOX
from the Bartolozzi Engraving of the Reynolds Portrait
made for Harding's "Shakspeare Illustrated"

THE FIRST AMERICAN NOVELIST?

By

Gustavus Howard Maynadier

 BOOKS FOR LIBRARIES PRESS
FREEPORT, NEW YORK

Copyright© 1940 by
The President and Fellows of Harvard College.
Copyright© 1968 by
The President and Fellows of Harvard College.
Reprinted 1971 by Arrangement with
Harvard University Press.

```
PR
3541
.L27   T 72 15436
M3
1971
```

INTERNATIONAL STANDARD BOOK NUMBER:
0-8369-6618-X

LIBRARY OF CONGRESS CATALOG CARD NUMBER:
79-175703

PRINTED IN THE UNITED STATES OF AMERICA
BY
NEW WORLD BOOK MANUFACTURING CO., INC.
HALLANDALE, FLORIDA 33009

THE FIRST
AMERICAN NOVELIST?

THE FIRST AMERICAN NOVELIST?

I

ABOUT 1740 there was a young woman in London, Charlotte Ramsay, hoping confidently to make a living by her pen, whom there is reason to call the first American novelist. For according to general belief she was a native of New York, where she was born in 1720 and where she lived till she was fifteen, when she went to England, to spend most of the remaining nearly seventy years of her life in London. A few years after her arrival there Samuel Richardson's *Pamela* was published, which he with good critical judgment called 'a new species of writing.' It was; and with it the English novel began that career which is still vigorous. Only ten years after *Pamela* this American young lady made her début as novelist with *The Life of Harriot Stuart*, in which for the first time in English fiction American scenes were presented by one who knew them at first hand. Be it ever so humble, the beginning of any important literary development must always be of interest. There is little question that one deserving the title of first American novelist should be American-born, should write about America, and should do so before any other novelist of American birth. Charlotte Ramsay, or Mrs. Lennox as she is generally known, seems to possess all these claims to the title. Yet paradoxically, though she achieved fame in London — Reynolds painted her and Johnson lauded her — no one knows who her family were.

Apart from her material and probable American birth, Mrs. Lennox deserves mention in literary history for appearing as a novelist so early. When *The Life of Harriot Stuart* (dated 1751 on the title page) was offered for sale in December, 1750, there were still but few specimens of the new fiction which had begun with *Pamela* in November, 1740. That, as everyone knows, had proved the spark to fire Fielding's genius to its characteristic brilliancy in *Joseph Andrews*. The two great founders of the English novel had followed their initial efforts with their masterpieces, *Clarissa* and *Tom Jones*. Just before these, young Tobias Smollett had produced a masterpiece of his own in *Roderick Random*. Gentle Sarah Fielding, the master novelist's sister, the not so gentle Mrs. Haywood, and Mrs. Joseph Collyer had essayed fiction during the decade. That was about all when Mrs. Lennox joined the ranks of novelists with her *Life of Harriot Stuart*.

But it is the newness of some of the material in this and of much in her *Euphemia*, forty years later — when, to be sure, it was not so new — which constitutes the chief interest of Mrs. Lennox. One does not meet the new material immediately on beginning the story which Harriot Stuart, Ulysses-like enduring of many adventures, writes at length to her 'dear Amanda' who has asked for the relation of her life, and whose 'request has always the force of a command with me.' Apparent, though, from the first is the precocity of the heroine, at twelve a prodigy of learning, an accomplished writer of verse, and already commencing breaker of men's hearts. After a first triumph of this sort in Westminster, her next was on the high seas, for her father, officer in the army and scion of a noble family, and also a man of the highest character, generally loved and revered, was 'preferred to a very considerable post in America'; a man-of-war was ordered to transport the Stuarts thither; and 'several gentlemen, whose affairs called them to that country, procuring a passage in the same ship, we had very agreeable company to soften the fatigues of the voyage.' Two of these gentlemen promptly fell in love with Harriot. One was a young Mr. Maynard, who 'had not only a very genteel fortune, but was lieutenant of a man of war; and, as he had great interest, was in daily expectation of being preferred to the command of a ship.' The other was a 'lovely youth' named Dumont (had Mrs. Lennox been reading Miss Fielding's *David Simple*, in part of which a Dumont is an interesting tragic hero?), born in 'N——,' the only son of one of its richest merchants, the adored of the 'languishing beauties' of that city, but unfortunately a 'papist' and from infancy betrothed to a cousin in England. For these reasons Maynard seemed to Harriot's parents the more desirable lover. Also on the ship was an amiable but rather indiscreet

FIRST AMERICAN NOVELIST? 7

and thoughtless young lady, 'the wife of one of my pappa's lieutenants,' who took a great fancy to Harriot, and who was to appear in a minor rôle later in the story. Thus early are suggested the possibilities in fiction of a trans-Atlantic passage, though the stilted language, the exaggerated sentiment, and the omission of common detail make Mrs. Lennox's narrative heavy and lifeless. The first few days out 'being extremely seasick, I was confined to my bed,' is about the only touch of realism in Miss Stuart's account of crossing the Atlantic.

'At last, after a tedious voyage of nine weeks, we came in sight of N——. That city making a delightful appearance from the water, I stood some moments contemplating it with great pleasure.' The Stuarts, apparently second only to the Governor's family in provincial rank, were received in great state, the Governor's coach waiting, when they landed, to carry them to their lodgings. As soon as they were settled, 'all the principal ladies of R—— came to visit us.' A succession of balls and other entertainments made the Stuart ladies hate to leave 'N——,' but the Colonel (that seems to have been the rank of Harriot's father) 'had determined to fix his residence at A——, a city near two hundred miles distant from —— ——, where he was to command in chief.' At their departure 'a great deal of company' saw the Stuarts off in their sloop, 'which was fitted up in a very elegant manner for our little voyage.' With a favorable wind, they 'reached A—— in two days, infinitely delighted with the prospect of several fine country-seats on each side of the river. My father was received with much respect by the inhabitants of A——, who had impatiently expected us. We were saluted by all the ships in the harbour, who had their flags and streamers out; and the mayor, with the principal persons of the city, waited our landing, and conducted us to the fort, in which was a very fine house, where the commanding officer always resided.'

There was to be plenty of excitement for Harriot in her new home. Stationed at the fort was the Governor's son, Captain Belmein, an ideally beautiful young man of twenty-four, who at once fell in love with her. So did an agreeable young surgeon who was presently sent to the post. Besides, there was always Maynard in 'N——,' threatening a visit, and strongly urged upon her for a husband by her mother and less strongly by her father. Nor could she forget Dumont, no less an Adonis or Apollo than young Belmein, who in spite of betrothal to his English cousin, had made his love for Harriot clear before she left 'N——.' Then there was a visit (Captain Belmein as escort) to the young married lady she had met on the ship, Mrs. Villars, whose husband was stationed at 'a village about twenty miles distant from A——,' the name of which was 'S——,' or as it occurs again, 'S——y.' Not far from that was a 'castle, as they called it,' of one of the Five Nations, and near that a fort 'to keep the Indians in awe,' commanded by another lieutenant of Harriot's father. Escorted by this officer Harriot visited several houses of the Indian chiefs and received many presents of their own making, though notwithstanding their conversion to Christianity, they appeared 'so savage and frightful' that she could hardly look at them without trembling.

Tormented by Belmein's ardent love-making, which was overcoming her inclination for Dumont, Harriot fell into a fever which caused her life to be despaired of. Belmein's anxiety left no doubt of his passion, and as soon as she was sufficiently recovered, he asked for her hand in due form. Mrs. Stuart did not approve; she had hoped to capture Belmein for her eldest daughter, her main reason for urging Maynard's suit on Harriot. But Colonel Stuart was persuaded to give his consent provided that the Governor made no objection to his son's choice. Unfortunately the Governor, notorious for his avarice, did object, because the Stuarts, though equal to the Belmeins in family, had no money. He ordered his son to 'N——' at once to join the expedition fitting out against Carthagena on the Spanish Main. The impetuous Captain tried to persuade Harriot to a secret marriage, but her father, whose pride was sorely hurt by the Governor's disapproval of the girl, made her promise never to marry young Belmein without the full consent of both fathers. At this juncture Belmein disappeared, having supposedly killed the young surgeon of the post in a duel.

The Governor was now expected shortly at 'A——' to meet the Five Indian Nations who came there every third year to renew their treaty of peace with Great Britain, and went away childishly happy in the possession of several hundred pounds' worth of presents bestowed on them by the British Government to make firmer their alliance. On the plain behind the fort they had already put up their huts of bark, with leafy boughs on the outside to protect them from the sun. Harriot, much interested in this newly arisen city, liked to view it from the garden, which was just outside of the fort. Walking there later than usual one evening, she was horrified to see four Indians rush through the gate, who seized her so suddenly that before she could scream for help she fainted. When she came to, she found herself in a boat rowing rapidly up a river. The oarsmen were Indians, their chief to her amazement Captain Belmein, whom presently the rising moon revealed dressed as one of them, frightfully painted face and all. He assured Harriot that she had nothing to fear. The rowers were Mohawks who were devoted to him, 'young men of quality in their own nation,' and all 'converted to Christianity.' Harriot, who never doubted her own charms, was pleased to hear these Christianised 'young men of quality' soon paying her 'complements in the Dutch language, which most of the Mohock Indians can speak fluently.' It was not such a bad adventure after all. She was comfortably wrapped in bearskins which her lover had provided (because 'after the excessive heats of the day,' summer nights in America 'are more pleasant and refreshing than can be well express'd,' with 'just coolness enough in the air to be agreeable'), 'the river we were upon is one of the finest in the world,' and there was light enough from the moon to show the 'romantic' and 'wild' beauty of the banks.

All night the Indians rowed with all their strength. The Captain explained that the abduction was to enable Harriot to marry him, as she had once inclined to do secretly, and so make herself safe forever from Maynard. But she was of a different mind now after promising never to marry Belmein without consent of his father as well as hers. Besides, his violence had alarmed her. She couldn't help wondering if he really intended marriage. So stoutly she insisted on the quickest possible return to her father that her lover agreed to deliver her at 'Fort H——,' apparently the fort which she had visited when staying with Mrs. Villars at 'S——,' from which she could easily return to 'A——.' But first he would take her to his brother's farm, which she had heard of as one of the best in the province, to consider there for a day or two whether after all she had better not forget her word and marry him.

Belmein's brother was most cordial and courteous in receiving Harriot; his farm proved all that she had expected. But her suspicions of the Captain grew through the day, and next morning when only a servant or two was up, she managed to make her escape to 'Fort H——,' from which she was sent to her father with a suitable escort. Captain Belmein raged, but notoriously fickle he soon regained his composure and was ready — no longer a fugitive because the young surgeon thought killed in the duel had only been wounded — to set out from 'N——' for Jamaica, thence presumably to take part in the British expedition against Carthagena, in which incidentally were to engage a very young surgeon in the British Navy, Tobias Smollett, and a gentleman not much his senior from the right bank of the Potomac, Lawrence Washington, who had a schoolboy brother whom the world was to hear of. About the same time the unfavored Maynard, convinced of the hopelessness of his suit, left for England to take command of the man-of-war to which at last he was appointed. So two overzealous lovers passed from Harriot's life.

Meanwhile Governor Belmein came to 'A——' for his meeting with the Five Indian Nations, and the town was in gala array. Though unwilling to have dowerless Harriot for a daughter-in-law, he was susceptible to her charms and assiduous in paying her court. The gentlemen who came with him from 'N——' followed his example, among them notably young Dumont. Harriot felt now more drawn to him than ever, but remembering his religion and his betrothal to the cousin in England she decided that he was 'too dangerously lovely' to admit much to her company. Even so, she was unspeakably gratified by his love-lorn sighs and glances.

Scarcely had the Governor with his train gone back to 'N——' when a short illness proved fatal to Colonel Stuart, and his wife and daughters were left sadly straitened. Having discharged most of their servants they went to 'N——,' uncertain whether to stay there or return to England. Harriot's brother found himself obliged to go to Jamaica because of business interests, and his parting with her, his favorite sister, proved so harrowing that she fainted in his arms. A sister of Mrs. Stuart's in England, the widow of a baronet, asked to have Harriot sent over to her in the spring, to be provided for as her own child. It was then the beginning of winter, and in the intervening months Dumont, though 'so much the darling of the ladies in N——, that it seem'd as if all their endeavours to charm were for him,' more and more showed his passion for Harriot. In spite of his religion and his engagement to his cousin, he won from her an admission of love, and the promise to remain unmarried and keep him in memory for one year after leaving him.

So the day for sailing came. Harriot's

parting with her younger sister, Fanny, was no less heart-rending to both than parting had been with her brother, but Fanny was 'a little composed' by her mother's promise to let her make a visit to the elder sister, now married, 'who lived in Philadelphia.' Harriot's farewell of Dumont had been two days before, and she could not bear the pain of another, but she left a letter for Fanny to give him. Then with her governess and very good friend, Mrs. Blandon, who was to see her safely delivered to her aunt, she took ship for England. Since Harriot's later adventures have little bearing on the claim of Mrs. Lennox to the title of American novelist, it is enough to give them as briefly as possible.

To begin with, Mrs. Blandon and her charge had been hardly ten days at sea when their ship was captured by a Spanish privateer. In only a few hours this in turn was captured by a British man-of-war, to which the ladies were transferred. The unprincipled captain, married man though he was, presently made proposals to Harriot to be his mistress, and followed them by attempted rape, from which she saved herself by drawing his hanger from his side and wounding him almost mortally. His nephew, a young officer named Campbel, also fell in love with Harriot, but the very opposite of his uncle, he guarded the ladies with the chivalric care of a knight of old. The one time that he becomes a real young man crossing the ocean with a pleasing young girl is when he calls Harriot's attention to 'the beautiful variety of colours which glittered on the backs of the Dolphins, that were sporting upon the surface of the sea.'

Arrived in England, Campbel insisted on escorting the ladies from Dover up to London to Harriot's aunt. But the aunt, because of a malignant fever, had gone incurably mad, her house was shut up, and she was in the country under the care of her brother-in-law. A neighbor and friend of the aunt, a Mrs. Dormer, who gave this information, took a great liking to Harriot, which was fortunate, for presently her dear friend and governess, Mrs. Blandon, died of small-pox; and curiously, in view of the high position of her family, she seemed to have no one in all England to turn to. Her aunt's brother-in-law, to be sure, sent her a present of a hundred pounds, but he showed no great desire to see her. Campbel importuned her to marry him, but she could not forget her promise to Dumont. Thanks to friends of Mrs. Dormer she was recommended to great patronesses, but they proved unreliable. Mrs. Dormer remained her one haven of refuge.

News from America was first bad and then good. Her beloved brother had died, and the shock of this intelligence threw Harriot into a sickness which made the physicians 'absolutely despair' of her recovery. But as she was convalescing a letter from Dumont raised her to ecstasy. In studying doctrinal books to convert her to catholicism, he had, 'to his great amazement and confusion,' converted himself to protestantism, and he was coming speedily to England to get his cousin to release him from his betrothal so that he might marry Harriot. He came; matters were arranged with the cousin; the wedding-day was set; but a villain uncle ('papist' of course) of the cousin made Harriot believe Dumont faithless. Then to prevent any reconciliation of the lovers, he abducted Harriot to Paris and

FIRST AMERICAN NOVELIST? 19

put her in a convent, declaring her his niece, to stay till Dumont should return to the faith of his fathers from which she had seduced him. Thanks to a kind elderly marquise who visited the convent, Harriot was able to send word of her situation to Mrs. Dormer. That lady and Dumont, whom she informed of the abduction, went to Paris, as it happened separately, to have Harriot released, but too late. She had already been taken from the convent by a young French count, who had escorted the marquise on several of her visits and had fallen in love with Harriot. By presenting a forged letter from the marquise he persuaded Harriot to let him effect her escape and drove her to his house at St. Denis, there to remain till she accepted his love. From this new abductor she escaped with the help of a jealous mistress of his, who burst into Harriot's chamber one evening dressed as a young man, of course causing Harriot almost to faint, but with no worse design than by exchanging clothes to hurry her rival out of the way.

Thus rescued from the count Harriot by happy chances got back to London, where she found that her mother and her sister Fanny, now married, and Fanny's husband had recently arrived from America. Campbel, too, was there, urging his suit as eagerly as ever; and finally, impelled by her family and still persuaded of Dumont's infidelity, Harriot agreed to the marriage. At that moment Mrs. Dormer, whose long absence had caused Harriot great concern, returned from Paris and assured her of Dumont's constancy. Harriot was in despair. She had the highest esteem for Campbel and the strongest love for Dumont. Sure that whichever she married, the other would die of a broken heart, she could only declare her resolve to remain single all her life. Fortune, however, made the two suitors into such fast friends that she felt safe after all to choose one. Dumont, back from France, came upon Campbel one night, on the road from London to Hampstead, just in time to save him from footpads who were about to overcome him, and Campbel swore 'to preserve an inviolable friendship for' his rescuer. He entreated Harriot to marry Dumont, as having prior claim to her hand, and was at their wedding 'with a serenity in his countenance, which persuaded' her that 'his heart was entirely at ease.'

Though this summary omits various incidents which further complicate the story, it is enough to show what a tangled web Mrs. Lennox was weaving in her first novel. It must make evident too that *The Life of Harriot Stuart* cannot claim the distinction of late so much talked of in the United States, and coveted, of being 'one hundred per cent American.' Mathematical calculation reveals that if the novel is to be judged 'American' by the number of pages in which America is the scene, it is only a fraction over twenty-six per cent so. At that it may be called timidly American, for Mrs. Lennox shows a curious unwillingness to give American places their full and undisguised names, though with one exception there is no doubt what they are. The city where the Stuarts land, the capital of the province, is always 'N——' or '—— ——,' but never New York. They sail up a beautiful but always unnamed river 'near two hundred miles' (which is about fifty too much) to live in the fort at 'A——,' but never at Albany. Thence Harriot goes to visit Mrs. Villars at

'S——,' or 'S——y,' a village some twenty miles away. When she escapes from the too ardent Belmein, she flees to 'Fort H——' on a second unnamed river. For some curious reason, the only place whose name Mrs. Lennox writes boldly out in full is Philadelphia. The younger sister, Fanny, was allowed by way of comforting her for Harriot's departure for England to 'make a visit to my eldest sister, who lived in Philadelphia.' It were idle to speculate on this sole dropping of disguise, however transparent, in Mrs. Lennox's American place names. There seems no reason to think that in her day the Quaker City enjoyed the reputation for somnolence and innocence which American newspapers and vaudeville 'comedians' not so many years ago were pleased to fasten upon it, a reputation, by the way, which those best qualified to know have declared in *both* respects totally unwarranted. However that may be, the fact remains that an estimable young lady in this novel of the middle eighteenth century counted it a privilege to make a visit in Philadelphia.

One place name only in *Harriot Stuart*

FIRST AMERICAN NOVELIST? 23

baffles identification, 'R——,' of which 'all the principal ladies,' including 'the governor's lady and daughters,' came to call on the Stuarts as soon as they were ready after their voyage to receive them. Unquestionably New York is where the Stuarts land and stay for a while, and where 'the governor's lady and daughters' reside, so the conclusion must be that 'R——' (which is never mentioned again) is a misprint for 'N——.' At first sight there may appear uncertainty about one other place, 'Fort H——,' though that might have been recognised more easily in 1750 than to-day as Fort Hunter near the confluence of the Mohawk River and the Schoharie, built there to overawe a Mohawk 'castle.' This site of the fort identifies the beautiful river up which Captain Belmein's Indians rowed Harriot with might and main as the Mohawk and not the upper Hudson, which one might at first think it. How many such identifications British readers of the time would make is a question, though except in the case of New York, it is doubtful if the real names would have meant much more to them than the disguised.

Yet if vaguely American, the pages which

are so deserve mention for being American so early. It is a safe bet that when Harriot Stuart stood some time 'contemplating with great pleasure' the 'delightful appearance' of 'N——' from the water, it was the first notice in English fiction of 'the New York skyline' which, either in books of travel or in novels, has impressed so many tourists of the twentieth century viewing it from incoming steamers. When Harriot made visits to 'S——' or 'S——y,' it was over a century and a quarter before Henry James sent Daisy Miller from Schenectady to Italy to die of 'Roman fever.' How many other heroines of English fiction, except a later one of Mrs. Lennox, Euphemia Neville, have been to Schenectady anyway? These facts add to the interest if not to the amount of the American percentage of Mrs. Lennox's first novel. But the letters which Harriot receives from America might be allowed to add a little to this amount. What is more, both her sisters, to the evident satisfaction of the family, marry in America, the elder, we know, a Philadelphian, but Fanny, perhaps one there only temporarily, for he was a gentleman who proposed to 'return' to England in a few months. About the 'lovely youth,' Dumont, however, there is no possible doubt whatever; he was born and brought up in New York. And when the heroine of a novel marries a New Yorker, that should add something surely, perhaps a good deal, to its American percentage.

Forty years later, at the age of seventy, Mrs. Lennox used what has usually been thought her native land for fiction again. The novel was *Euphemia*, and American scenes form a much larger portion of it than of *Harriot Stuart*. If the author, as generally stated, went to England at fifteen, it was fifty-five years since she had looked on them. If she was older, as may be possible, authentic mention of her in England makes it at least some forty-five years since she had seen them. So the novel gives proof again of the lasting strength in many people of childhood impressions, and also of the tendency with the passing of years to magnify them.

The story is told by the exchange of letters, which with a few exceptions are written by two devoted friends, Miss Maria, later Mrs. Edward Harley (she married her cousin), and Mrs. Neville, formerly Miss Euphemia Lumley. Each lady tells her own story, and Maria Harley's is the better in plot, which is distinct if conventional. Euphemia Neville's, however, is the better in human interest, at times showing no little skill in characterisation, or at least in conception of character. As Miss Lumley she is virtually forced into marriage, after her father's sudden loss of property and death, by the desire of her dying mother to see her well provided for by marriage with Mr. Neville. He is a fine figure of a man, of good impulses and at first sight 'something very gracious and insinuating in his manner.' About thirty years old, of good family, and heir to a wealthy uncle, he seems to Mrs. Lumley an ideal husband for a penniless daughter, and for the short time she lives after his marriage, he is a devoted son-in-law. But there is another side to his nature. As one who knows him describes him to Maria Harley, he can be 'the worst-tempered man in the world,' extravagant, self-willed, conceited. Loving Euphemia as truly as he can anyone, he is yet a domineering husband, expecting abject obedience, who cannot appreciate her finer qualities. She soon understands his failings perfectly, she realises her mistake in marrying him, but she has given her troth, he is the father of her children whom he loves in his own selfish way. Whatever is fine in him she can admire, and she is conscientiously a good wife. That is all the plot there is to Euphemia's story — one of the best women in the world married to a man with certain good qualities, who in his bullying self-importance never understands the treasure he has in her.

Neville's nature being what it is, it is not surprising that soon after marriage he has run through most of his money, and what little Euphemia had too. Seeing no way to restore his fortunes while waiting for his rich uncle to die — who happens to be in the best of health — but service overseas, he gets an appointment as 'first Lieutenant to one of the independent companies in New-York,' and when the novel begins he and his wife are making preparations to be away from England for an indefinite period. Maria Harley, who has been in France and has not seen Euphemia since her rather sudden marriage, has nevertheless heard of Neville's plans, and writes to her friend that she cannot bear to think of her 'doomed to waste' her days in America. This, as early as the third page, strikes the keynote of the heroine's own story. It deals mostly with her experiences in America, more her impressions of the new land but not without mention of her marital trials, till she returns to England only a few pages before the end.

Though Maria implores her friend not to cross the ocean with the ill-tempered Neville to live in 'unknown regions,' but to stay with her till his service in America is over, Euphemia feels it her duty to go. From this point much of *Euphemia* is *Harriot Stuart* over again, but with more definiteness and detail. Colonel Bellenden, Neville's superior officer, and his wife and three daughters bear a striking resemblance to the Stuart family. Like Colonel Stuart, Colonel Bellenden, equally lovable, commands the fort at Albany, now only a hundred and fifty instead of two hundred miles up 'Hudson's River,' as Mrs. Lennox always calls it, from 'New-York,' invariably hyphenated. The voyage to Albany, made in three luxuriously appointed sloops which accommodated the whole party, began with a salute of canon from the Battery as the Colonel's sloop passed, and 'the ladies of the fort family (for that is the phrase here)' coming out and waving their handkerchiefs. It lasted eight days, protracted so long because the travellers always dined on shore, and at any time when they wished to explore the country they had the skippers come to anchor. This gives Mrs. Lennox a chance to paint the crudities of the lesser Dutch farmers along the river, which she does in a way that must have interested Washington Irving if he read her book, as he might well have done, being of an age to read novels a few years after it came out. She is impressed, too, as they float 'down' — not up — the 'most delightful river imaginable,' by the beauty of the shores, sometimes all 'wild and romantic, sometimes with flourishing plantations, and elegant mansions.' The passage through the Highlands, though she doesn't call them so, makes a particular impression. The river, very narrow at that point, runs between mountains whose sides are 'adorned with the most beautiful verdure, and trees of many species unknown' in England. The 'awful gloom from the surrounding shades, the solemn stillness, inspired a soft and pleasing melancholy' in the party, who were, 'as the poet says, "Rapt in pensive musing." '

Arrived at Albany Mrs. Neville has experiences very like Harriot's in the earlier novel, except that Harriot was the young daughter of the commanding officer at the fort, and Euphemia is the young wife of one of the commanding officer's lieutenants. And nobody abducts her, that fashion at the end of the century being in favor chiefly for the heroines of Gothic Romance, which *Euphemia* for the most part is not. Mrs. Neville gives a more particular account of Albany than Harriot did — a place 'worse built' than New York, with few of the houses presenting a good appearance outside, though 'an excessive neatness reigns within.' The ladies of the leading families call on the ladies of the fort, but without much pleasure on either side, for while the Dutch can all speak English they are shy about using it, and the English ladies generally know no Dutch at all. Besides, the dress and talk and manners of the Dutch are so uncouth as often to create disgust, and when the English ladies return their calls they are expected to partake heartily of the veritable collation which their hostesses offer. Their own 'thin European regale of a dish of tea, and a slice of cake' must seem stingy, Euphemia thinks, to the Albany ladies accustomed to their full afternoon repasts.

In New York no 'savages' are ever seen, but they are a familiar sight in Albany, where the Indian trade is the most important industry. The Indians will walk into any house if the doors are open and make themselves at home, and one morning Euphemia is alarmed to find an Indian sitting by the fire in her kitchen, horrible in his red, yellow, and black paint and powder and enormous barbaric ornaments. Yet like Harriot, she is interested to visit the Mohawks' 'castle,' and she writes at length of their manners and customs, and of the Governor's meeting at Albany with the chiefs of 'our good allies, the Iroquois.' The Indians gather in numbers as Harriot described them, and their departure, after their usual presents of 'blankets, hatchets, iron-kettles, glass jewels, and the like,' 'no one regrets.'

'Dear Maria' in England 'can have no conception of the rigor of a North American winter.' The snow may lie five feet deep, frozen so hard as to feel like solid earth. The Hudson is 'become an icy plain; and bears on its frozen bosom deep loaded carriages, called sledges, drawn by horses, which seem to fly over the glassy surface.' For five months 'no abatement of this extreme rigor' is to be expected. The first time Mrs. Neville drives through the snowy woods, a 'furious bear' following the sledge is just ready to spring upon its occupants when a gentleman of the party brings it down with his gun.

At the beginning of another winter the Nevilles and two or three friends came near dying of starvation and cold. They set out from Schenectady, the ladies in a coach and Mr. Neville and a servant on horseback, to spend a day or two at a place ten miles away which a lady of the party had just bought. They had gone hardly three miles when it began to snow, but Mr. Neville, the invariably right, declared it was too early in the season for a heavy snowfall, and in spite of remonstrances from all the others, insisted on pushing on. The snow continued, harder and harder, and after the first night at the newly purchased house, the party found themselves with roads impassable for a coach, and snow so deep and soft that a man attempting to walk would sink in up to his waist. It was bitter cold, there was very little fuel and very little food. Fortunately for the visitors a drunken Indian came along, fell in the snow not far from the house, overcome with rum, and died, and Neville, who by his obstinacy had got the party into their desperate situation, put on the Indian's snowshoes and so made his way to Schenectady, from which he returned with a sledge and rescuing soldiers.

This is after Neville's appointment to the command of a fort at 'Schonectady,' as Mrs. Lennox spells it – in *Harriot Stuart*, be it remembered, never more than 'S——y.' Inconsiderate of his wife's feelings as usual, he has insisted on going there for the gratification of 'being greatest where all is little,' though to Mrs. Neville it is virtually going out of the world. For this 'little town, distant about thirty miles from Albany' — in *Harriot Stuart* it was distant about twenty — is 'inhabited only by some Dutch traders. Seldom visited by any strangers, but Indians, who straggle hither, not only from the five nations of the Iroquois, our allies, but the savages of Canada, and other barbarous nations.' No language but Dutch is spoken. But 'the country about is romantic and picturesque.' On a preliminary visit to see what Schenectady was like, the Nevilles made an excursion to 'the Falls of Cohas' (Cohoes), a 'cataract . . . in the river Mohawk before it falls into Hudson's river,' whose beauty stirs Euphemia to highest enthusiasm. Another time they go in canoes upstream to Fort Hunter, delighted with the romantic shores and the beauty of the 'verdant mountains.'

During the thirteen or fourteen years that the Nevilles remain in America, Mr. Neville, always liking amusement, gets leave from time to time to visit Boston, Philadelphia, and other places; but it would seem that Euphemia never leaves the province of New York. She is once on the point of going to Philadelphia with Colonel Bellenden's family, all agog to see 'that celebrated city,' for whose founder she has the highest admiration, when to the sorrow of all who know him a paralytic stroke takes the Colonel's life as suddenly as 'a short illness' in the earlier novel took Colonel Stuart's. By this time her sojourn in what Maria Harley had called 'unknown regions' was about over. Neville's rich uncle, reflecting that he was now eighty-one, decided to settle half of his estate on his nephew and pay his passage and his family's back to England. So Euphemia's banishment ended.

The Nevilles had two children, a boy named Edward and a girl three years younger, and a bit of conventional romantic fiction is introduced into the story of this boy. When he was three, he and a man-servant of his father's were seized near the Falls of Cohoes by a party of Huron Indians on their way home after selling furs to the English settlements, and taken to Canada. The servant was forced to live with the Indians, and the boy was turned over to the Jesuits' College in Montreal, where he was brought up under a sort of guardianship of the Father Rector, who hoped to make him into a priest. But after nine years or so the servant escaped, went to Montreal and found Edward out, telling what family he came of, and the French authorities sent the two to Oswego, whence Edward could be returned to his parents. Neville had already gone to England, but Euphemia had been obliged to delay her return and so she could welcome her restored son back to his birthplace. The familiar device of a birthmark did yeoman's service more than once in identifying Edward, but now a birthmark of good North American brand. For it was a bow and arrow under his left breast, caused by the fright of his mother shortly before he was born at meeting in the woods three drunken Indians, their leader armed with a bow and arrow, who for a time seemed dangerous.

Besides her two novels with American scenes Mrs. Lennox wrote three, perhaps four, others, of which far and away the best is *The Female Quixote: or, The Adventures of Arabella*, her one work still interesting by virtue of intrinsic merit. Published only a year and a quarter after *Harriot Stuart*, it is so superior to that effort as to seem hardly by the same hand. Indeed if *The Female Quixote* were sufficiently shortened, it would be not merely good but very good. No wonder Jane Austen admired it, as her letters show, for it has scenes of excellent humor and a situation which she thought fit to duplicate in *Northanger Abbey* — a lovable young girl absurdly misjudging everyday happenings because she views them in the light of the preposterous romances which she has read. Only Lady Arabella, the heroine of *The Female Quixote*, knows even less of life than Miss Austen's Catherine Morland and reads romances even more extravagant, with the result that her fantastic ideas, unlike Catherine's, often go too far beyond probability. Yet Mrs. Lennox builds a good foundation for her heroine's conceits. She is the only child of a marquis who from being the most powerful minister in the kingdom was banished the court through plots of his enemies, and misanthropically retired to a castle of his in a remote county. His wife died after giving birth to their daughter and

Arabella grew up the greatest lady of the neighborhood, yet knowing of human beings hardly any but her father and his servants, and her father died when she was barely seventeen. Of books, though, she knew more than enough, for in the castle was an ample library of which Lady Arabella had the range, and her favorite reading was in the colossal French romances of the seventeenth century. From these she constructed a world of her own as fantastic as Don Quixote constructed from *his* books. Every personable young man she meets she thinks so deep in love with her at first sight that when discouraged, as according to rules of romantic etiquette he must be, his ardor may at any moment turn him into a ravisher. She thinks it only courtesy on meeting a lady for the first time to beg for the story of her life, which may prove embarrassing if that life has not been all that it should be. Haymakers in the fields she takes for enemies of her cousin, a champion ready to shed his last blood in her defense. A tipsy strumpet at Vauxhall dressed in boy's clothes she takes for a great lady involved in some 'very notable adventure.'

Always she justifies her conduct by citing examples of Thalestris Queen of the Amazons, Parthenissa, Statira, Parisatis, Clelia, Cleopatra, Mandane, or some other incomparable heroine of her romances. Curious situations arise because of her hearers' ignorance of these ladies or ideas about them radically different from hers. On one occasion, in flight from her castle because of a supposedly too ardent lover (in reality a gardener) who may carry her off and keep her in chains, she implores a young gentleman in a chaise driving by on the road, in the name of her he loves best to help her. Nothing loath because of her beauty, he is ready to do all he can, till unfortunately she speaks of illustrious ladies before her who had been carried away, as Parthenissa and Cleopatra, and held captive by their ravishers. Parthenissa, the gentleman exclaims, he has never heard of, nor of more than one Cleopatra ' "but she was never ravished, I am certain, for she was too willing." ' This is too much for Arabella who believes Cleopatra, deriving her ideas from La Calprenède's *Cléopâtre*, an immaculate but much injured angel, lawfully married first to Julius Caesar and afterwards to Marc Antony.[1]

' "How, sir? . . . was Cleopatra ever willing to run away with her ravisher?"

"Cleopatra was a whore, was she not, madam?" said he.

"Hold thy peace, unworthy man," said Arabella, "and profane not the memory of . . . that queen . . . whose courage was equal to her beauty; and her virtue surpassed by neither. Good heavens! what a black defamer have I chosen for my protector!" '

So the young gentleman in the chaise is incontinently deprived of the honor of knight errant so recently conferred on him.

At the same time there passes from the picture the young man who innocently enough starts the adventure in which the Egyptian paragon of courage, beauty, and virtue is calumniated. He is Edward, an under gardener of sufficiently good looks and address to persuade Lady Arabella that he is a great personage who descends to menial service because of love for her. If

---

[1] It is not the renowned Queen who is the heroine of the romance, but Princess Cleopatra, her daughter by her second *husband*.

he leans against a tree when he ought to be working, it is because he is dreaming of her. If he has taken a string of small pearls which she left one day in an arbor, it is to keep it for secret adoration. Though she fancies that he sighs when he meets her, she cannot understand why he never carves her name on trees with cryptic expressions of love, nor why her maid Lucy never takes him for anybody but a simple gardener. He rises high in the lady's esteem one day when she discovers the head gardener beating Edward and peremptorily bids him desist, whereupon Edward sneaks away. He was stealing carp from the Marquis's fish-pond, the head gardener says, no doubt to sell, but Lady Arabella knows better. He had gone to the pond in despair to drown himself. A day or two later Edward leaves her father's service — to avoid a shameful dismissal, the other servants say, but Arabella understands perfectly that having failed of an opportunity to declare his love, he has gone away to plot means of carrying her off. That is why, when he comes back after her father's death to beg to be restored to his old position, she is panic-stricken at sight of him and flees, as we know, only to be overtaken by him after she has met the young gentleman in a chaise. The more he protests his desire to be the best of servants to her, the more she commands him to banish himself from her sight. He shall trouble her ladyship no more, he says finally, crestfallen and entirely perplexed, for he remembers her kindness when the head gardener was beating him. 'But I think it hard to be punished for a crime I was not guilty of,' is his parting remark, his mind still on the carp. A rogue of some promise this Edward, the only remarkable one that Mrs. Lennox drew, and one that either of her contemporaries, Fielding and Smollett, would have made much of.

Unfortunately few other characters of *The Female Quixote* have equal reality. One is the maid Lucy, a Sancho Panza changed in sex and some other respects to suit the conditions of Mrs. Lennox's novel, accepting as gospel her mistress's strangest opinions, and because of them in continual bewilderment. Arabella herself critics have generally praised for her womanly reality, not of the first order surely, yet enough to make her a lady of true delicacy, lovable and charming in spite of her illusions. In this she resembles her literary successor already mentioned, Catherine Morland, and in some ways, too, another novel-reading young lady, Lydia Languish. She is further like Miss Languish in her repugnance to accepting a husband who has been picked out for her — in each case the hero of the tale — and also, it may not be too trifling to observe, in having a maid named Lucy, though the two Lucys have nothing in common. Other characters occasionally gleam into reality, but the majority are lifeless, even the hero for the most part, exemplary and sensible young man though he is, and admirably patient with the vagaries of his lovely cousin whom he finally marries.

A serious fault of the novel which commentators have pointed out is the clumsy way in which at last Arabella's conversion to good sense is brought about. It is chiefly by the arguments and exhortations of a dry-as-dust parson in the longest chapter of the book. Probably the dullest too, despite Mrs. Lennox's entitling it, 'Being in the author's opinion, the best chapter in this history.'

Dr. Johnson, it seems probable, wrote most of the chapter because of his high regard for Mrs. Lennox; and it was a sign of her high regard for him that she not only entitled the chapter as she did, but also inserted a clause in one of the sentences, referring to him as 'the greatest genius in the present age.' A still graver fault of the novel is the length. Arabella's incessant pointing to the behavior of her favorite romantic heroines becomes tedious in the extreme. If all her adventures, which vary in interest greatly, had the interest of the best, there would still be too many. And too many, as already remarked, are beyond the bounds of probability. Even so, Macaulay was not justified in declaring that if we consider *The Female Quixote* 'as a picture of life and manners, we must pronounce it more absurd than any of the romances which it was designed to ridicule.'[1]

Such a charge might with much more reason have been brought against *Harriot Stuart* which, with its bewildering mass of improbabilities, seems at times almost burlesque. Obviously Mrs. Lennox never so

[1] *Madame D'Arblay*, Edinburgh Review, January, 1843.

intended it. All seriously she sought to portray her Harriot as a thoughtless girl whose coquettish vanity was the cause of many of her trials, yet gifted and affectionate, with generous feelings, and finally sense enough to laugh at her youthful folly. To this study of character, unskilful and almost buried out of sight by Harriot's adventures, Mrs. Lennox had the originality to add those scenes based on her own experiences in America which constitute the novelty of the book and its greatest interest. Only Mrs. Lennox herself had read too many romances; *The Female Quixote* shows that at one time she must have been a prodigious reader of them. *Harriot Stuart* was her first novel, and the art of the new kind of fiction — character more important than adventure — was itself young. Mrs. Lennox was still too near lifeless, formless models. She never learned to write a compact story, she never attained complete reality of characters or scenes, but after her first experiment she did make an advance in her second novel, later by only fifteen months, that is marvelous. If she never wrote so well again, she was at least able to give considerable reality to the beginning of *Henrietta*, her third novel, and in *Euphemia*, when she was seventy, to rouse some interest by phychological study.

II

Yet it is *The Life of Harriot Stuart* and not its entertaining successor which, so far as is known, gives the first outward and visible sign of the admiration for Mrs. Lennox cherished over years by Dr. Johnson. He was pleased to call it her 'first literary child,' and it was to celebrate its 'birth' that he insisted not long after its publication on having the famous all-night party, chronicled by Sir John Hawkins,[1] at the Devil Tavern. The guests numbered between twenty and thirty, all men (one being Mr. Lennox) except Mrs. Lennox 'and a lady of her acquaintance, now living'; the hour of assembling was eight; the supper was 'elegant,' and not the least part of it 'a magnificent hot apple-pye,' stuck with bay-leaves because Mrs. Lennox had written verses. Also there was a crown of laurel with which Johnson, with 'ceremonies of

[1] *Life of Johnson*, 1787.

his own invention, encircled her brows.' Though the only beverages — at least the only ones mentioned — were coffee, tea, and lemonade, and though at last sleep began to get the better of the 'pleasant conversation' and the 'harmless mirth' which the company enjoyed, it was not 'till near eight' in the morning that the party broke up.

More than thirty-three years later Johnson 'in fine spirits' remarked to Boswell and others 'at our Essex Head Club' that he had dined the day before with Mrs. Garrick, whose other guests were Mrs. Carter, Hannah More, and Fanny Burney. Then he went on to the panegyric of Mrs. Lennox which may be all that many readers of Boswell know of her. 'Three such women are not to be found,' he declared, and he could think of no fourth worthy of them 'except Mrs. Lennox, who is superior to them all.' Amiable and gentle as she was, Fanny Burney could not let this pass unnoticed as she wrote her *Diary*. She takes pains to say that she had been obliged to explain the remark to a gentleman whom it had filled with astonishment as he read Boswell's *Life*, then just published, for 'he had never even heard' of Mrs. Lennox. She made quite clear to him that only the few who knew Johnson well were aware of 'the power of the moment over his unguarded conversation' and 'how little of his solid opinion was to be gathered from his accidental assertions.'[1]

Even so, there is abundant proof of his high and steady regard for Mrs. Lennox from the night of the party in her honor at the Devil Tavern, when he was forty-one, to the day in May of his seventy-fifth year, only seven months before his death, when he pronounced the encomium on her which Miss Burney had to explain. He wrote the Dedication of her *Female Quixote* to the Earl of Middlesex and probably, as has been noted, the longest, and dullest, chapter of the book; and in many other ways he helped her from time to time in her literary ventures. He took her to call on Richardson, though to be sure, as Fanny Burney is careful to remark, at her own request.[2] He paid her the compliment in his Dictionary of

---

[1] *Diary and Letters of Madame D'Arblay*, Macmillan, London, 1904-05 ed., Vol. IV, p. 477. The fact that the gentleman alluded to was a foreigner probably had something to do with his ignorance of Mrs. Lennox.

[2] *Id.*, I, 86.

quoting *The Female Quixote* to show the proper use of the word *talent*. He praised her in conversation and in letters. And a letter from her to him shows that they were on terms of such pleasant familiarity that he might go to her house to eat either the apple-dumplings or the gooseberry tarts which she took pride in making.[1]

If we seek the reasons for this regard they are not hard to find. Johnson was by no means an infallible critic, as many of his literary judgments prove, and not least his crowning Mrs. Lennox with laurel before, instead of after, she had written *The Female Quixote*. Her first novel warranted no such honor, and before that she had published only a few verses which long since died the death they deserved. But Johnson was a zealous moralist, and seeing the clumsy moral in *Harriot Stuart* he overlooked its artistic weaknesses. Similarly in Mrs. Lennox's slender production of poems he saw and admired her moralising, however conventional and sentimental. He may have been pleased too by a general stiff correct-

[1] Miriam Rossiter Small, *Charlotte Ramsay Lennox*, New Haven, 1935, p. 50.

ness of the verse and occasional splightliness of thought. Also there were other than literary reasons, and better founded, which would make a special appeal to him. Mrs. Lennox was a young woman honestly toiling to make a living, an eager student if not really a scholar, tireless and courageous in the face of difficulties and disappointments. Of these latter, failure to succeed on the stage was one, for Horace Walpole in 1748 records seeing her in a play at Richmond and finding her a 'deplorable actress.' Present knowledge permits only conjecture in regard to other troubles, but there is evidence that they came to her early. In 1754 Fielding writing the Introduction to his *Journal of a Voyage to Lisbon* mentions 'the inimitable and shamefully-distressed author of the Female Quixote'; Richardson, praising her in a letter to Lady Bradshaigh, a year or so before, says she 'has been unhappy.'[1] Neither hints at the cause or nature of her afflictions, though Fielding's reference to them suggests that they were well known. No doubt lack of money was

[1] Mrs. Barbauld, *The Correspondence of Samuel Richardson*, London, 1804, Vol. VI, p. 243.

one. Whatever they were, to a man of Johnson's chivalry and sympathy and sense of justice they would be only further reasons for warm esteem.

Now this rugged moralist, it is to be remembered, was a good deal of a philanderer, and Mrs. Lennox was an attractive woman. Her portrait painted by Sir Joshua Reynolds when she was about forty shows her a lady of considerable beauty, not lacking in character, with an alert expression suggestive of a sly, perhaps roguish sense of humor, one might say a little arch. She might very well be interesting to talk to. Yet the fact that she and 'a lady of her acquaintance' were the only women in the party at the Devil Tavern suggests that she was more a man's than a woman's woman. That may be why contemporary praise of her is all from men, why we never hear of an intimate woman friend of hers, unless possibly Mrs. Yates, the actress, whom she seems to have known better than any other woman. (Could Mrs. Yates have been the one other feminine guest at the Devil Tavern party, 'now living' when Hawkins was writing his *Life of Johnson*? She did not die until 1787.) Five or six ladies — three of them of the greater nobility — at various times gave Mrs. Lennox material aid, but it would seem from admiration and compassion rather than affection, and with two of them she appears to have quarreled. Mrs. Thrale, initiating Fanny Burney into high literary society, told her that though Mrs. Lennox's books 'are generally approved, nobody likes her.'[1] Even Johnson's admiration did not win her invitations to Streatham.

There is no suggestion that eighteenth century ladies fought shy of Mrs. Lennox because of doubts about her family and station, and yet perhaps they might have been justified in entertaining them. For the only detailed and careful study of her ever made, *Charlotte Ramsay Lennox — An Eighteenth Century Lady of Letters*,[2] by Professor Miriam Rossiter Small of Wells College, a book of highly valuable information, gives the impression that Mrs. Lennox was willing to have her family believed of more consequence than it was. She seems to have

---

[1] *Diary and Letters of Madame D'Arblay*, Macmillan, London, 1904–05 ed., Vol. I, p. 86.
[2] New Haven, Yale University Press, 1935.

spoken of it very little, and not always with the most scrupulous truth. But America was so far away, to many another world, that without enquiring too closely people accepted her story as she told it, that she was daughter to the 'Royalist Governor' of the province of New York, where she was born in 1720, and that his death, about the time she went to England to live, had deprived her of means of support. Certain influential ladies consequently befriended the rather mysterious American girl when — perhaps not yet twenty — she began her struggles to make a living either on the stage or by her pen. Somehow she struggled on, still unknown to fame, till at the age of twenty-seven, apparently in the year of her marriage to one Alexander Lennox, she had her first book published, *Poems on Several Occasions*. From that time till past middle age she was more and more in the public eye, but as a literary rather than a social figure.

Of those who knew her, some, Richardson among them, knew Mr. Lennox too, but more did not; he seems to have been merely the husband of his wife, and at times a burdensome one. We have no hint of any child of the couple till a daughter was born when they had been married seventeen years and a half and Mrs. Lennox was forty-five — a circumstance, by the way, which no one who has written of her has ever mentioned as at all singular. A year or two later there was a son whom his mother refers to apologetically in a letter to Johnson, when she was fifty-seven, as a little boy noisy and troublesome. He was still young enough for her to call him in a letter sixteen years later, when she was seventy-three, an 'unfortunate youth,' a term more likely to be applied by a woman of that age to a grandson than a son. Meanwhile her books, as we know, were 'generally approved,' and despite Mrs. Thrale's remark to Fanny Burney, there were those who did like her. To some of the younger generation she was doubtless an object at once of wonder, reverence, and compassion. For she came from strange, remote New York, of which her father was reputed to have been Governor; she had the prestige of being a pet of Dr. Johnson and the author of the celebrated *Female Quixote* and other works; and when past seventy she merited particularly the title, which Fielding had given her when little more than thirty, of 'shamefully-distressed.' She was alienated from her husband some years before he died; her son had got into trouble which made it necessary to send him out of the country; her health was failing and her money gone; and her daughter had died, 'the only friend she had a claim upon.'[1] But three or four friends, young enough to be her children, came to her aid, and with the help of the Literary Fund, a society established in 1790 for the benefit of indigent authors, secured for her at least creature comforts till her death on the fourth of January, 1804.[2] Early biographical notices state that she was eighty-four years old, which, if taken literally, means of course that she was born on one of the earliest days of the year.

All notices of Mrs. Lennox from the first have dealt much more with her works than with her life, for the very good reason that information about her works was so much the easier to obtain. In regard to both there

[1] Miriam Rossiter Small, *Charlotte Ramsay Lennox*, New Haven, 1935, p. 61.
[2] Nichols, *Literary Anecdotes*, London, 1812, III, p. 201; and later notices of Mrs. Lennox.

have been misstatements, especially — as Miss Small's researches prove — in the very little related of her life, which is almost all untrustworthy. Mrs. Lennox herself, we have seen, appears, at least partially, responsible for the scanty information and the errors in the early accounts of her. The latest of these based on reports of persons who had, or might have had, acquaintance with Mrs. Lennox is Croker's note about her in his edition of Boswell's *Johnson* (the eleventh of that famous biography) in 1831, when he repeats Sir John Hawkins's story of the party at the Devil Tavern. He says that his information comes from 'the Right Hon. Sir George Rose, whose venerable mother still remembers' Mrs. Lennox. Inasmuch as Sir George Rose's father, who died in 1818, only fourteen years after Mrs. Lennox, was one of the friends who assisted her most in her last years and was, according to Croker, 'at the expense of her burial,' it would seem that information given by his son and his widow was what they, rightly or wrongly, believed accurate. Prior to Croker's there were some half dozen biographical notices of Mrs. Lennox, none much longer than his. The earliest, an obituary notice, appeared in *The Gentleman's Magazine and Historical Chronicle* for January, 1804, the month of Mrs. Lennox's death. There is, too, the meagre information in the records of the Literary Fund, presumably furnished by herself when she was recommended to the managers of that institution for aid, that she was the 'daughter of Colonel Ramsay, Royalist Governor of New York in 1720,' and that she was born in New York that same year.

With the exception of Croker's, which has marked differences, these early accounts of Mrs. Lennox are very much alike. They are all based on the obituary notice in *The Gentleman's Magazine*, which they copy, sometimes verbatim, but more often with slight changes in wording and content. What these articles have to offer may be judged from a summary of the one in *The Gentleman's Magazine*.

Mrs. Lennox, says the notice, was 'a lady of considerable genius, and who has long been distinguished for her literary merit. She may boast the honour of having been the *protegée* of Dr. Samuel Johnson and the friend of Mrs. Yates.' Then after a sketch, not always accurate, of her literary work we learn that her father was 'a field-officer, lieutenant-governor of New York, who sent her over at 15 to a wealthy aunt, who desired to have her, but who, unfortunately, on the arrival of her niece, was out of her senses, and never recovered them; immediately after which the father died, and the daughter from that time supported herself by her literary talents, which she always employed usefully.' Her 'latter days' were 'clouded by penury and sickness,' calamities 'in a considerable degree alleviated by the kindness of some friends, who revered alike her literary and her moral character.' Among these it would be unjust not to mention 'the Right Hon. George Rose and the Rev. William Beloe.' But the most effective help came from the directors of 'that truly-useful and highly-important institution, the Literary Fund; by whose timely aid her only son was, a few years since, enabled to fit himself out for an employment in the American States; and by whose bounty the means of decent subsistence have, for the last twelvemonth, been afforded to the mother.'

This earliest account of Mrs. Lennox, it may be observed, does not name New York explicitly as her birthplace, though it implies that it was. It does not give her father's name — he is nothing more definite than a 'field-officer' and 'lieutenant-governor' — nor does it tell whether she had brothers and sisters. It mentions no child of hers except the son, though some later accounts speak of her daughter. Three or four, like *The Gentleman's Magazine*, make no mention of the father's surname and one or two repeat in almost identical words its story of the son's being enabled by the Literary Fund to fit himself for employment in America. What this was they do not say, nor what his reason for leaving England, but that it was distressing a letter of Mrs. Lennox of August twenty-second, 1793, makes all too plain. She is begging for aid from the Literary Fund because she sees 'an only child upon the brink of utter ruin.' He was driven 'to desperation by a most unnatural father, and then deserted, and left exposed to all the evils that may well be expected from the dreadful circumstances he is in.' She would save him if she could; but in vain, she says, she has tried 'to raise money to send this unfortunate youth to my relations in the United States of America, who will receive him kindly.' Unless the money is forthcoming soon, he will not be able to sail 'till next March.'[1] The Literary Fund accordingly paid Mrs. Lennox twelve guineas 'for the express purpose of enabling her to send her son to Virginia, and thence to Baltimore, where the young man's friends reside.'[2] Later one more guinea was given 'to cover additional cost of passage of her son to America.'

'Colonel Ramsay,' we have seen, Mrs. Lennox's father is designated in the records of the Literary Fund, though in the periodical and encyclopaedic articles about her, he is at first only a 'field-officer' without stated rank, or even surname. Sometimes when not mentioned this last is implied in the statement that his daughter's maiden name was

---

[1] The letter is quoted by M. R. Small, *Charlotte Ramsay Lennox*, New Haven, 1935, p. 59.

[2] *Id.*, p. 57. While it had been known at least since the first biographical notice of Mrs. Lennox, in 1804, that the Literary Fund had helped her, details of their relations were not made public till the Society gave them to Professor Small for use in her book.

Ramsay.[1] In Chalmers's *General Biographical Dictionary*, 1815, he is not only 'Colonel' but also 'James' Ramsay, the first time we have his given name. Croker likewise has him 'Colonel' but not 'James.' In Nichols's *Literary Anecdotes*,[2] when Mrs. Lennox's name for once becomes 'Barbara-Charlotte,' he is promoted to 'General' Ramsay. After his appearance in the Literary Fund records as 'Governor' of New York, he is never more than 'Lieutenant-Governor.' Who his wife was we never hear. The sole reference to that lady is in Chalmers's *Biographical Dictionary* (whose article on Mrs. Lennox seems rather better considered than any of these others) which says that Colonel Ramsay left his widow, like his daughter, 'without any provision,' and that she died in New York in August, 1765. If that is so, for perhaps thirty years after Charlotte Ramsay went to England her mother was alive, and yet no hint has been found that she ever spoke of her to English friends.

[1] The first two notices fail to give even this. She is only "Mrs. Charlotte Lennox."
[2] Vol. VIII (London, 1814), p. 435. This is supplementary to the account of Mrs. Lennox, *id.*, III (London, 1812), pp. 200–201.

While some of these early notices of Mrs. Lennox make no mention of her husband nor others of her son, they generally accord her the honor of having been the *protégée* of Johnson. Three or four speak of her as the friend of Mrs. Yates and two as also a friend of Richardson. The phrase in *The Gentleman's Magazine*, 'lady of considerable genius,' is repeated more than once. We are told invariably that the English aunt to whom Charlotte Ramsay was sent, was 'unfortunately' out of her senses on the girl's arrival, till we come to Chalmers in his *Biographical Dictionary* in 1815, who seemed to think it superfluous to designate losing one's senses 'unfortunate.' Of the more obvious errors in these accounts is the statement of *The Lady's Monthly Museum*, June, 1813, that it was after *The Female Quixote* came out that Mrs. Lennox was introduced to the great Doctor; it was the year before, we know, that he arranged the celebration of the 'birth' of her 'first literary child.' The same periodical has Charlotte Ramsay married to Mr. Lennox 'at a very early age,' a phrase hardly justified, since evidence points to her being twenty-seven at the time. The only other information it gives of her husband, is that he was 'a gentleman in a public office.'

It is Croker in 1831 who tells us most of the husband, and that is not much.[1] Probably about 1747, he says, Charlotte Ramsay, whose volume of poems had recently come out, 'became acquainted with and married a Mr. Lenox (*sic*), who was in' the employ of William Strahan, the printer, 'but in what capacity is not known.' The Duchess of Newcastle, a kind patroness of Mrs. Lennox, got him 'the place of tidewaiter in the Customs.' Croker adds that nothing more is remembered of Mr. Lennox, 'except that he, at a later period of life, put forward some claim to a Scottish peerage.' All this, coming to Croker, as he says, from his friend Sir George Rose, whose father did so much for Mrs. Lennox and whose mother remembered her, may be authentic, but his remark that Mrs. Lennox 'is said to have been very plain in her person' surely records a mistake. The Reynolds portrait is suf-

---

[1] Note to Hawkins's account of the supper at the Devil Tavern, Croker's edition of Boswell's *Johnson*, I, p. 208.

ficient answer, even allowing for flattery, which it is said often crept into Reynolds's pictures of women. Yet it must be remembered that Sir George Rose's father was twenty-four years younger than Mrs. Lennox, and that when he befriended her, time and worries might have changed sadly the woman whom Sir Joshua painted when she was forty-one.

Subsequent articles on Mrs. Lennox have been too late to benefit by the knowledge of any one acquainted with her. They have not all been animated by conscientious scholarship. It seems pure fancy when we read, without any citation of authority, that Charlotte Ramsay acquired her education 'in the best schools of the city of her birth' (who knows what it was?), for 'her father's position gave to the child unusual advantages.' It is manifest error when we read that Mr. Lennox died shortly after *Harriot Stuart* was published, which was in 1750, for his daughter was not born till 1765, and his son a year or two later. All in all, even after Miss Small's investigations, not much is known of Mrs. Lennox except as a woman of letters. What Chalmers's *Biographical*

Dictionary stated as far back as 1815 seems true to-day: — 'very little is known of her early history,' for the few friends who survived her 'became acquainted with her only in her latter days.'

Such being the case, it is doubtful if we shall ever know just who Charlotte Ramsay Lennox was. It would be interesting if we could follow in detail her course from an uncelebrated girl in the province of New York to the woman of letters whom Johnson admired. No doubt it would show courage and capability. But our definite knowledge of her earlier life is almost nil and that of her later years meagre. It may be said almost with certainty, however, who she was not; and that is, daughter of a 'Royalist Governor' of the province of New York, who held office in 1720. In that year William Burnet, subsequently transferred to Massachusetts, was the only governor, and before he assumed office in September, Peter Schuyler, President of the Council of the colony, had been acting governor. Other governors of the province during Charlotte Ramsay's supposed residence there were John Montgomerie, who immediately succeeded Burnet, and then William Cosby, with one Rip van Dam, senior member of the Council, acting governor in the interval between them. Sometimes there was a lieutenant-governor, but his office seems not to have been made permanent till the 1750's, when Mrs. Lennox was already a celebrity in London. Of the few holding that office earlier in the century no Ramsay is recorded. Apparently Mrs. Lennox was stretching the truth when she allowed the managers of the Literary Fund to name her father in their records 'Governor of New York.' Apparently, too, without any qualms she had allowed people in general to believe him either governor or lieutenant-governor. It would be interesting to know whether she led Johnson to think so, but as to that no evidence has been found one way or the other.

If Mrs. Lennox misrepresented the position of her family in New York, and if people believed her misrepresentation, can we be sure that she told the truth about her birthplace? Could she have been born in Great Britain after all, in which case she cannot be called the first American novelist?

A reason for such suspicion is her reference in *Harriot Stuart* to the 'delightful appearance' of New York from the water. She would have been more likely to mention this, one might think, if her first impression of it had been, like her heroine's, after a 'tedious voyage' from England rather than a diminishing picture as she sailed away. Again, so far as she gives life to her two American novels, the voyage out from England is more real than the voyage back — in *Euphemia* considerably so, for one sentence suffices to take Mrs. Neville home over the sea, whereas twenty-seven pages are devoted to taking her to New York, with some little detail of the weather, and once the excitement of seeing a huge iceberg. Would this be so if Charlotte Ramsay's first and only experience of the ocean was in a crossing which took her away from her native land to a new one, keyed to excitement and wonder of what the new land might give?

The answer is that it is no greater feat of the imagination than Mrs. Lennox's novels show her abundantly capable of, to fancy the 'great pleasure' with which a young girl would contemplate the little eighteenth-century city of New York from the water after nine weeks at sea. Custom could never stale the impressiveness of New York harbor, and Mrs. Lennox in her girlhood may have admired the 'skyline' of the colonial metropolis more than once as she returned from some little water excursion. Or she may have got her first sight of it from the Hudson after coming down the river from Albany, where there is reason to think that she may have been born. No early mention of her birthplace suggests that 'New York' may not mean the province rather than the city, and in the notice of her in *The Lady's Monthly Museum* (June, 1813) it apparently does. As to the ocean voyages, if there is a wee bit of reality in the iceberg of the western crossing in *Euphemia*, so there is in the colors on the dolphins' backs in the eastern crossing in *Harriot Stuart*. Finally, what reason would Mrs. Lennox have had to name America as the land of her birth, if it had not been? If she came of a family in England which for some reason she was ashamed to acknowledge, one of those who according to Mrs. Thrale did not like her would surely have ferreted it out, in spite of the subterfuge of American birth. If she came of an English family which she was not ashamed of, there would have been no reason at all to call herself an American. It is inconceivable too, in such a case, that there should have been none of the family to help her in her troubles, that nobody who writes about her mentions relatives of hers in England. The only ones she ever mentions herself lived in Baltimore.

Charlotte Ramsay's sad experience when she arrived in England of finding her aunt 'unfortunately' — and what was worse, permanently — out of her senses, of unaccountably having no one else to turn to, and so being obliged to support herself, is all so like part of *Harriot Stuart* that this part has been supposed autobiographical. However that may be, there is little doubt about autobiography, barring the love affairs, in the American portion of the story. Harriot saw in America what in all probability her creator herself had seen — life in the outposts of the colony rather than in the capital. If Charlotte Ramsay's father like Harriot's had the rank of colonel it would seem to have won him no higher position than Colonel Stuart's, and afterwards Colonel Bellenden's in *Euphemia* — commanding officer of the fort at Albany. But instead of being colonel he may never have been more than lieutenant or captain. Though Professor Small, as she shows in an appendix to her *Charlotte Ramsay Lennox*, has made exhaustive search through army lists and state papers for Mrs. Lennox's father, she has not been able positively to identify him. Perhaps she restricted herself unduly in confining her search to a Ramsay named James, for only one early account of Mrs. Lennox so designates the gentleman. But even of James Ramsays it appears that there were in His Majesty's Province of New York about 1720 some half dozen of proper age for fatherhood, who were then or later officers in the army. None of them was of higher rank than captain. Mrs. Lennox's naming her father a colonel would seem as unveracious as her naming him a governor or lieutenant-governor.

After all, stories long accepted often have some foundation even if slight, and by connecting those reported of Mrs. Lennox with both the few facts known of her and the autobiographical suggestions in her novels, it is possible to construct a history of her that may not be far from truth. The date assigned for her birth, 1720, seems entirely probable. It would make her in the twenties when she published her first book and when Horace Walpole thought her a deplorable actress. It would make her thirty when she was writing her first novel, and it is not likely that when the new kind of fiction was so young a woman under thirty would dare try it. Sarah Fielding, the first English woman who did, was thirty-three when she wrote *David Simple*, and she had the shining example of her brother to encourage her. New York as the place of Mrs. Lennox's birth seems equally probable, though as we have seen, 'New York' is an equivocal term. There is no doubt that she knew well certain aspects of life in the province of that name. No one who did not could have written with the detail in both *Harriot Stuart* and *Euphemia* of its Dutch as well as English society, of the Indians of the Five Nations and their meetings with the English governors, of Albany and the country and rivers round about. She appears to know that region of the province so much better than any other — there is never the detail about the city of New York, for instance, that there is about Albany and Schenectady — that it is almost safe to say that in or near Albany she was born.

Whether her father was then in the army, or a civilian who received a commission later, he must some time have been stationed at the fort at Albany long enough for his daughter to know intimately the life of that post. Probably, like Mr. Neville in *Euphemia*, he was stationed at Schenectady too, and possibly at Fort Hunter. It would have been remarkable for a woman writing in London when *Clarissa* and *Tom Jones* were new to send her characters to such rough little frontier outposts unless she knew them well. It is even conceivable that in whatever capacity at such places, her father may, for some brief moments, have had reason to assume enough gubernatorial authority to make it not too hard for a feminine conscience later to speak of him as 'Governor.' Finally, there can be little doubt that for part of her girlhood the Commanding Officer at Albany was a gentleman whom the Ramsay family loved and venerated, with qualities like those of Colonel Stuart and Colonel Bellenden in the novels.

After Charlotte Ramsay went to England, it is not so easy for a time to reconstruct her life. The earliest biographical notices say that her father 'sent her over at fifteen' to the English aunt, but they are so often mistaken that she may not have gone till she was older. There are even reasons to make a later age probable. It would account for observation of American scenes sometimes rather mature for a girl under fifteen, and it would shorten the mysterious veiled period of twelve years in England when she was said to support herself by her writings, not one of which is known till the end of that period. Perhaps the war with Spain, which began in 1739, had already been declared when she crossed the ocean, and fears of passengers may have suggested the episode in *Harriot Stuart* of the Spanish privateer. She may even have remained in America till the expedition against Carthagena was fitting out, which Captain Belmein left Albany to join. She would have been then only twenty, and perhaps might have passed for less and been willing to. There is a suggestion that she looked young for her age, for Richardson reported her twenty-four in a letter to Lady Bradshaigh when actually she was thirty-two.[1] Of course the younger a girl was thought who worked valiantly for a living, the more interesting and admired she would be. Was there a time when Mrs. Lennox misrepresented her years, as she did her father's rank and dignity?

In view of the resemblance between what are reputed Miss Ramsay's first experiences in England and those of her first heroine, the question naturally arises how much does *Harriot Stuart* at this point mirror struggles of the author, and how much have commentators ascribed to the author difficulties which she gave her first heroine? At least they had in common the lack of near relatives which is so surprising in view of the position which Mrs. Lennox gave to both the Stuart family and her own. Mrs. Lennox, like Harriot, had high-born patronesses

---

[1] Mrs. Barbauld, *The Correspondence of Samuel Richardson*, London, 1804, Vol. VI, p. 243.

whose favor she did not always retain. Both were obliged to work for a living, Mrs. Lennox always though Harriot only temporarily. Resemblances cease when with the appearance in 1747 of *Poems on Several Occasions* Charlotte Ramsay's life as a woman of letters becomes well marked. But there is still the mystery of her private life. Why nothing of the family of this attractive-looking, almost (according to engravings of the Reynolds portrait) beautiful young woman? She must have been at least fairly well connected, or she would not have secured her high-born patronesses. Her writings show that in spite of occasional bad grammar she was well educated, that she was acquainted at once with fashionable society and good artistic society, indeed (again Mrs. Thrale and Miss Burney to the contrary notwithstanding) with some of the best literary society of the day. How much Johnson esteemed her we know. 'Her moral character . . . was never impeached.'[1]

Yet relationless in England, as she appears to have been, she evidently kept up a correspondence with her family in America

---

[1] Croker's Boswell's *Johnson*, London, 1831, I, p. 208.

which even the Revolution did not break. Otherwise she could not have written so confidently to the Royal Literary Fund in 1793 that her relatives in the United States would receive her ruined only son kindly. At least since Johnson's first laudation of her more than forty years earlier she had been before the public, but no writing known of all those years gives a hint that she had kept any connection with the land of her birth. And it is possible that for part of this time her mother was living in New York! America she could not have been ashamed to own as her native land, for besides so naming it, she made use of it in her first novel and again in her fifth. But something made her secret about her family there. If illegitimacy had been the reason, scandal must surely have made it known. We can only conjecture that though probably well born, her family were not of a position to make her anxious to acknowledge them, still less proud of them, as doubtless she would have liked to be. And so the fiction of the 'Royalist Governor' or the 'field-officer, lieutenant-governor of New York.' It makes us think of Mrs. Rawdon Crawley and her noble Gascon ancestors, who grew in rank and splendor as Becky progressed through life. But nobody has ever suggested that Mrs. Lennox was an adventuress, and evidence points to the contrary. There is something sly, though, in the expression that Sir Joshua gave her. There is meaning in that concise statement in the notice in Chalmers's *Biographical Dictionary* only eleven years after her death — 'very little is known of her early history by her few surviving friends.'

Further conjecture would be that Charlotte Ramsay, like Harriot Stuart, had a sister who married in Philadelphia. Thence children of hers, and she perhaps with them, might easily have made their way to Baltimore, where the unfortunate Lennox son was to take refuge after leaving England. Of course there might have been other Ramsay sisters with children, and also brothers, who lived in Baltimore or Philadelphia, or in New York where one account says that their mother spent her last days. It would not have been surprising if some of them had made known their near relation to Mrs. Lennox in a way to get itself recorded. The author of *The Female Quixote* and other novels, of *Shakespear Illustrated* (even if hack work which did her little credit), of a few plays, and of several widely read translations from the French, was a sister or a cousin or an aunt worth claiming. But no information has ever come from relatives in America about the Ramsay family, nothing to fix Mrs. Lennox in any square of kinship. Even now it seems as if some might be obtained, for as late as 1793 there were the relatives in Baltimore, probably near ones, of the Ramsay blood if not also of the Ramsay name. There might perfectly well be descendants of theirs to-day who could recall family traditions of Mrs. Lennox and her parents and their children.

If there are, they should let them be known. Mrs. Lennox was enough of a personage to make additional information about her to be desired. Though mostly without conspicuous literary merit, her works were nevertheless esteemed in her day; and *The Female Quixote*, admired by many a critic, still has life. She played a remembered part, if a somewhat mysterious one, in that eighteenth-century London society which lives

NEW YORK FROM THE SOUTHWEST, 1735

By courtesy of the Library of Congres.

in the letters and memoirs and biographies of the time. And she is memorable as the first, in all probability, of American birth to put American scenes, however far from vividly, into a novel — the little provincial capital of 'delightful appearance from the water' which has become the metropolis of a continent, the great river flowing down to it, forts and trading-posts on the rude frontier.

A brave soul, too, even if we think her foolishly secretive and misleading about her family in New York, for in the hard-pressed siege of adversity it was long before she would capitulate. A marriage that did not turn out well, sorrow in her children, always new schemes and new exertions to earn the necessary money — that was her life. It would seem that at times she had to be the support of husband and children both. Her pen was her whole equipment; she worked with it as long as her health lasted. If she did breathe the divine afflatus too seldom, let us at least not forget the words of *The Gentleman's Magazine* just after her death: 'her literary talents . . . she always employed usefully.'